# Rigby
# Pebble Soup Letter Kits

Blackline Masters

Rigby

EARLY CHILDHOOD

Pebble Soup

LITERACY RESOURCES™

**Pebble Soup Letter Kits**
**Blackline Masters**

06 05 04 03 02 01    10 9 8 7 6 5 4 3 2 1

© 2001 Rigby,
a division of Reed Elsevier Inc.
500 Coventry Lane
Crystal Lake, Illinois 60014

Executive Editor: Diane Dzamtovski
Design Project Manager: Judy Tresnowski
Design by Biner Design
Story Illustrations by Becky Radtke
Alphabet Illustrations by Roger Radtke
Photos by Bill Burlingham

Printed in the United States of America        ISBN 0-7635-7550-X

Visit Rigby on the World Wide Web at
**http://www.rigby.com**

# Table of Contents

# Assembling the Little Books

1. Photocopy pages 2/7 on the back of page 8/cover; photocopy pages 4/5 on the back of pages 6/3.

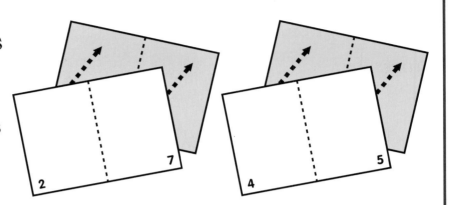

2. Place pages 4/5 on top of pages 2/7.

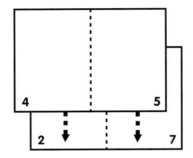

3. Fold the story in half so that pages 4/5 face each other and the cover is on the outside.

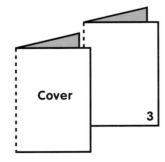

4. Staple the book together along the outer left edge.

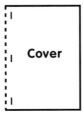

# Letter Home

Hello, Family!

Your child has brought home a Pebble Soup Letter Kit book for the family to share. The title of the book is _____.

We are working on learning the sound of the letter ____ and words that have this letter's sound. Learning the sounds that letters make is an important step in learning to read. You can help your child with this work. Here's how:

- Read the book together. Look for the featured letter and point it out.

- Have a letter treasure hunt. See who can be the first to find three things whose names begin with the featured letter.

- Make up a name for a doll or toy that begins with the featured letter. Help your child write that name on a piece of paper.

- When you take a walk or a drive, look for signs and other print that include words with that letter sound.

- Make up silly songs or rhymes that include words with the letter sound. For example, "Annie Alligator acts angry in the afternoon."

Please let me know if you have any other ideas that I could share with other families. Have fun!

# Alice Alligator

Name _____

Do you want to be an
actor one day?
Alice Alligator can show
you the way.

8

5

Alice Alligator likes to act.
She's quite good and
that's a fact.

2

She can act sad.

7

6

She can act angry.

**4**

She can act anxious.

---

She can act glad.

**5**

# Baby, Baby, Baby

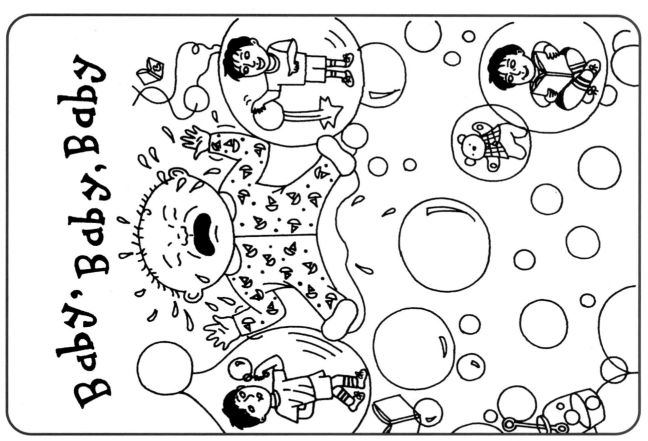

Name _____

---

Baby, baby, baby
Maybe, maybe, maybe
You won't stop crying at all.

**8**

9

Baby, baby, baby
Maybe, maybe, maybe
You would stop your crying . . .

2

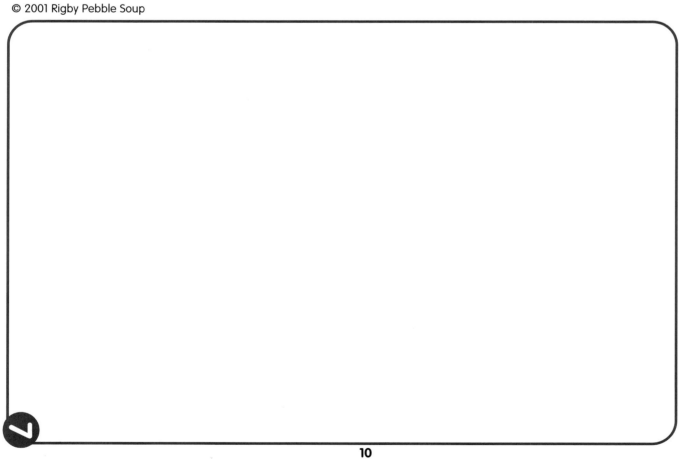

7

10

3

If I bring a book.

6

11

If I blow a bubble.

If I bounce a ball.

# Caroline the Cooking Cat

Name

13

She's making cupcakes
for you and me.

8

**2**

Caroline the cooking cat –
She puts on her cooking hat.
She counts out eggs –

---

one, two, three.

**7**

one, two, three.

She counts out
cups of flour –

**4**

She counts out carrots –

---

one, two, three.

**5**

# Dinah's Desk

Name _____

Now Dinah's desk has no
more places.
Now Dinah's desk has no
more spaces.

**8**

**2**

Dinah's desk has many places.
Dinah's desk has many spaces.

and dinosaurs, too.

**7**

3

For dishes and dolls

6

For doorbells and ducks

and trucks that are new.

# Elephants Everywhere

Name _____

and enjoyed themselves.

**8**

21

Elephants, elephants
everywhere

The elephants did . . . .

22

"Ride the elevators," said the elves.

**4**

Carrying eggs up and down the stairs.

**5**

# Fay
## the Firedog

Name _____

25

She jumps on every fire truck.
It's quite a sight!

**8**

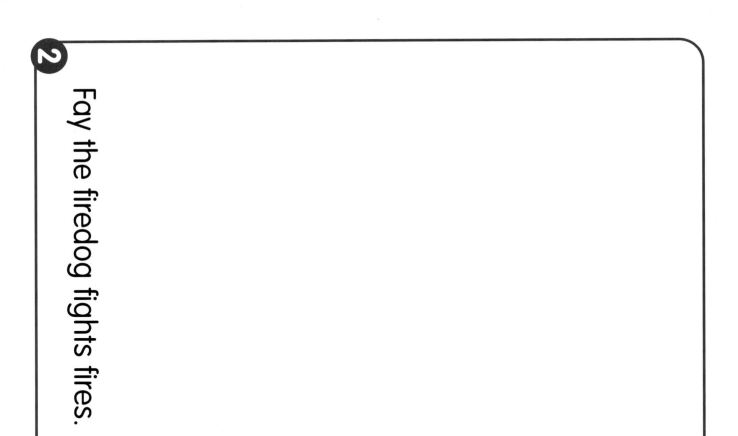

Fay the firedog fights fires.

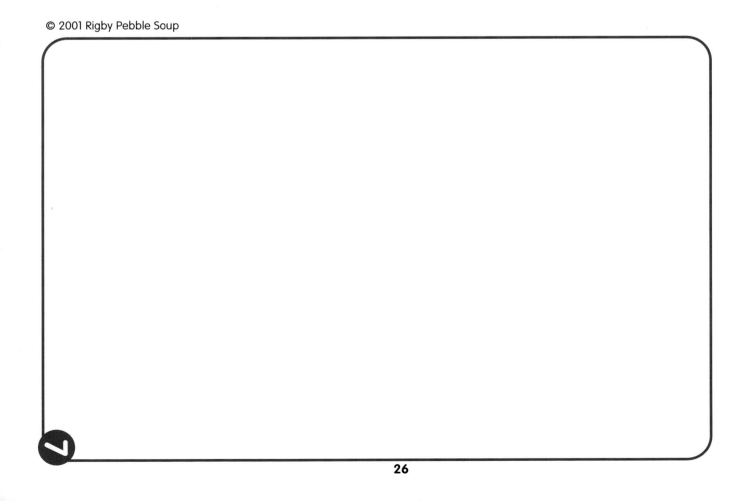

Fay the firedog never tires.

3

---

She's at the firehouse
Morning and night.

6

27

**4**

Across the field
She'll fetch a ball.

Over a fence
No matter how tall.

**5**

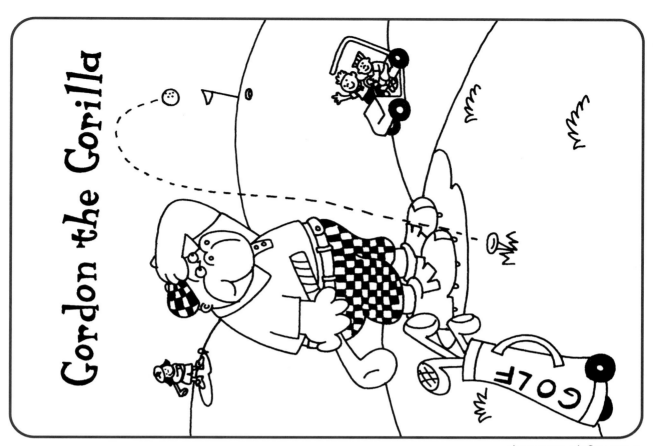

Gordon the Gorilla

GOLF

Name _____

"Can you guess where it falls?"

8

29

Gordon picks up his golf club.

"My goodness," he says.

He gets ready to play.

3

Here goes," Gordon shouts as he hits the ball.

9

31

**4**

"Golf is my game.
I play every day.

**5**

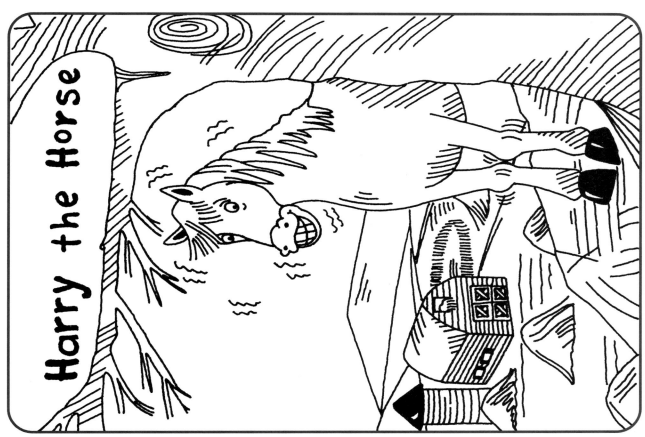

Harry the Horse

Name _____

With heat and hay and
everything else,
It's better than this tree.

**8**

I'm Harry the horse and I need some help. Won't you please help me?

2

---

That barn is right for me.

7

I hope, I hope,
I find a house.

6

**4**

I need a house to keep me warm.

---

It's cold here under this tree.

**5**

# Invitation
## to an Igloo

Name _____

'Cause it's in an igloo.

8

37

**2** I got an invitation to a party.

**7** We're all dressing warm.

It's written in ink.

3

Itchy the insect is going
And the inchworm is, too.

6

39

**4**

I'll go with Iggy the iguana.

I think I'll wear pink.

**5**

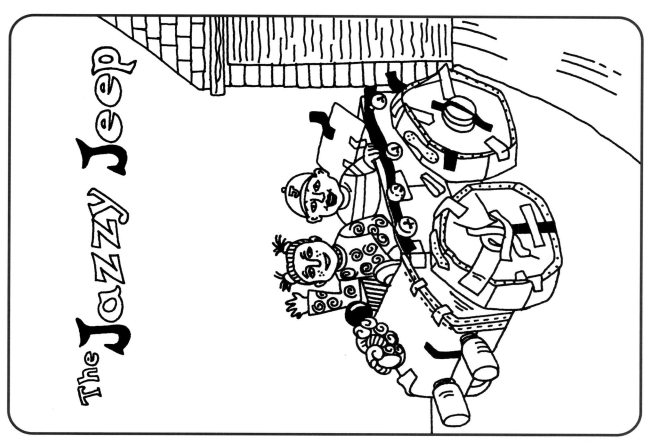

# The Jazzy Jeep

Name _____

and a horn made of shells.

8

41

**2**

It's jazzy.
It's snazzy.

It's got jumbo wheels

It's made out of junk.

**3**

and jingle jangle bells.

**6**

It's perfect for a journey,
And it's even got a trunk.

**4**

It's got jelly jar lights

**5**

44

# Ms. Kinkle at School

Name _____

---

We said good-bye to
Ms. Kinkle
And Kate out in the hall.

8

Ms. Kinkle read a story
All about a king
Who had a kite, a key,
And a magic yellow ring.

**3**

And then we played kickball.

**6**

We drew a little kitten

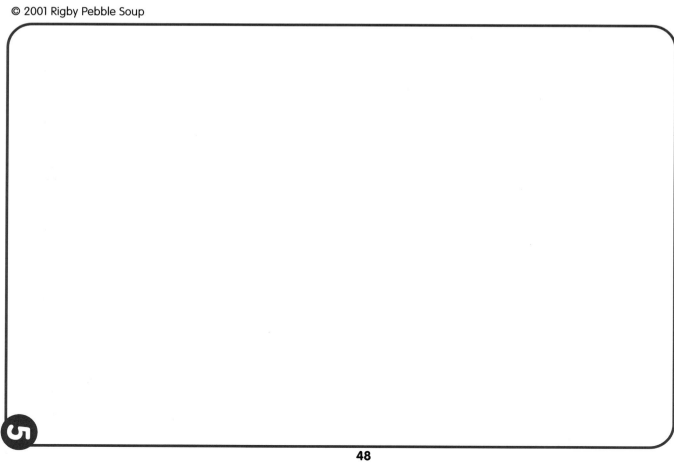

# Leo and Lyle

Name _____

---

Lyle builds lunches.
He makes them quite good.

**8**

49

Leo builds ladders.
He makes them quite strong.

2

7

3

Lyle builds, too.
But he doesn't use wood.

6

**4**

Leo builds ladders.
He makes them quite long.

**5**

# More Than the Man in the Moon

Name _____

---

Look up once and then
once more.
It's magnificent.
Wouldn't you say?

8

2

Look for the man in the moon
Up in the moonlit sky.

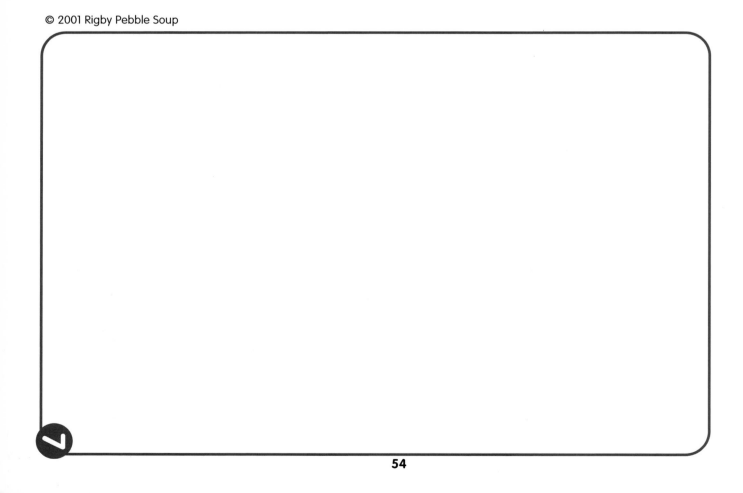

7

**3**

Millions and millions of stars
Make up the Milky Way.

**6**

**4**

Look for the planet Mars.
Go ahead. Give it a try.

**5**

# Nice Newspaper Stories

Name _____

---

What's it about? What do you suppose?
Well, I'll tell you. It's all about my nifty nose.

**8**

**2**

Newspaper stories in the news today —

---

And one about me.

**7**

Have you read them all?
What do they say?

**3**

There's one about nails

**6**

**4**

There's one about nine nests

In a big oak tree.

**5**

60

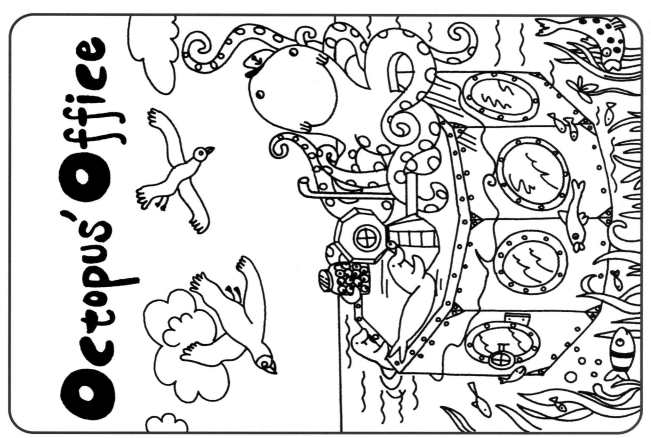

# Octopus' Office

Name _____

To eat olives in her office by the sea.

8

61

**2**

The octopus built an octagon office by the sea.

and otters

**7**

3

Inviting ospreys

6

63

4

In October it was done.

In November she had fun

5

# Aunt Peggy's Pigs

Name _____

---

See poodle puppies and pets galore.

**8**

**2**

Aunt Peggy's farm is a great place to be.

**7**

Wait! There's more.

Would you like to take
a look with me?

**3**

See pumpkins everywhere.

**6**

**4**

See Mama Pig and her piglets four.

---

See ponies peeking through a barn door.

**5**

# The Queen's Quilt

Name _____

'Cause it's her nap time.

8

2

Please be very quiet.

She's looking for her quilt . . . .

7

Please be very still.

3

I'll bet you a quarter.
I'll bet you a dime.

6

71

**4**

The queen is coming
Quickly up the hill.

---

**5**

# Rain, Rain, Rain

Name _____

Rain, rain, rain
Leaves a rainbow
by my door.

8

73

**2**

Rain, rain, rain

Rocks my paper rowboat.

**7**

Races down my window.

3

Rain, rain, rain

6

Rain, rain, rain

Makes the river roar.

# A Sunny Song

Name

And with that I can't go wrong.

8

77

2

These seeds will grow

As I plant some seeds

7

In the sunny sun

So I'll sing this song

4

If I sing a sunny song.

5

# Talking on the Telephone

Name _____

Talk, talk, talk, talk, talk . . . .

**8**

81

82

Talk, talk, talk, on
the telephone
today and every day.

There are tons and tons
of things
that I have yet to say.

**3**

Did I tell you about my
new toy truck?
Did you say no?

**6**

**4**

Did I tell you about taking turns playing tic-tac-toe?

**5**

# My Umbrella

Name _____

---

I've looked everywhere for my umbrella.
Now where can it be?

**8**

2

Have you seen my umbrella?

---

And up in the tree.

7

It's nowhere to be found.

**3**

I've looked up in the attic

**6**

4

I've looked upstairs
and downstairs

And even underground.

5

# Varooming in My Van

Name _____

---

Varoom!

8

89

**2**

Varooming through
the village,
Watch my van go.

And I shout out hi!

**7**

My van can go fast.
My van can go slow.

I see the vet and all
my neighbors . . . .

6

**4**

I see Mrs. Sweeny's vegetables . . . .

As I varoom by.

**5**

# Walking with Wanda

## with Wanda

Name _____

And a wasp that stings.

**8**

93

2

As Wanda walks
She sees a worm
that wiggles . . . .

7

94

**3**

As Wanda walks
She sees a spider's web . . . .

**6**

**4**

And a fly with wings.

**5**

# X Marks the Spot

Name

X marks the spot
As we exit.

**8**

2

Put an X on the box.

Put an X on the hook.

7

**3**

Put an X on the book.

**6**

**4**

Put an X on the fox.

**5**

Yancy the Yak

yodele yodele yoohoo

Name _____

Once you know how
to yodel,
You can yodel wherever
you go.

**2**

Yancy the yak learned how to yodel.

Yancy can teach you, you know.

It wasn't easy, you know.

**3**

Do you want to know how to yodel?

**6**

Once Yancy the yak
learned how to yodel,
He yodeled wherever
he'd go.

## A Zebra Named Zelda

Name _____

Z is the sound
that I like the best.

**8**

105

I'm a zany zebra named Zelda.

It's a sound with zest.

3

It's a sound with zip.

6

**4**

Z is the best sound I hear.

**5**

## a words

all
am
and
as
ask

## -at words

<u>at</u>
bat
cat
fat
hat

## -ax words

<u>ax</u>
sax
tax
wax

## b words

back

best

big

book

but

## -all words

<u>ball</u>

call

fall

hall

tall

## -ug words

<u>bug</u>

dug

hug

mug

rug

## c words

cake

came

can

car

cat

## -ake words

bake

<u>cake</u>

lake

make

take

## -an words

<u>can</u>

fan

man

pan

ran

## d words

desk
did
do
dog
doll

## -ip words

dip
hip
lip
ship
trip

## -uck words

duck
luck
cluck
stuck
truck

## e words

egg
elf
ever
every

## -end words

bend
<u>end</u>
mend
send
spend

## f words

fan
fat
fine
fish
fix

## -ell words

bell
<u>fell</u>
tell
well
yell

## -ight words

<u>fight</u>
light
night
right
bright

## g words

girl

give

go

good

great

## -ame words

came

game

name

same

tame

## -oat words

boat

coat

goat

oat

float

## h words

he
her
here
his
hug

## -ide words

<u>hide</u>
ride
side
wide
slide

## -ill words

fill
<u>hill</u>
<u>will</u>
chill
still

## i words

I

if

in

is

## -ink words

ink

pink

sink

wink

think

## -it words

fit

it

hit

sit

quit

## j words

jeep

joke

just

## -ump words

bump

dump

jump

lump

pump

## -unk words

bunk

junk

sunk

skunk

trunk

## k words

keep
kick
kind
kit
kitten

## -ing words

<u>king</u>
ring
wing
sing
bring

## -ite words

bite
<u>kite</u>
white
write

## l words

like
light
little
long
look

## -ap words

cap
lap
map
nap
clap

## -ate words

date
gate
late
hate
skate

## m words

many

mice

mine

more

my

## -ay words

day

<u>may</u>

say

way

play

## -eat words

beat

heat

<u>meat</u>

neat

seat

## n words

nine

no

not

now

nose

## -ail words

mail

nail

pail

sail

tail

## -ice words

dice

mice

nice

rice

price

## o words

on
open
other
over

## -old words

cold
gold
hold
<u>old</u>
told

## -ot words

dot
got
hot
not
spot

## p words

pet

pick

pig

play

put

## -in words

<u>pin</u>

tin

win

grin

skin

## -op words

hop

<u>pop</u>

top

shop

stop

## q words

quick

quiet

quit

## -ack words

back

pack

black

quack

track

## -ick words

kick

pick

sick

quick

trick

## r words

read

red

ride

ring

run

## -ain words

main

pain

<u>rain</u>

drain

train

## -ock words

lock

<u>rock</u>

sock

block

clock

## s words

said

she

sing

stop

sun

## -ale words

pale

tale

<u>sale</u>

<u>scale</u>

whale

## -aw words

jaw

paw

<u>saw</u>

claw

draw

## t words

take

talk

tell

to

two

## -ank words

bank

sank

<u>tank</u>

drank

thank

## -ore words

more

sore

<u>tore</u>

wore

store

## u words

under
until
upon
use

## -up words

cup
pup
<u>up</u>

## -us words

bus
<u>us</u>
plus

## v words

very

vest

van

## -ane words

cane

lane

mane

vane

plane

## -ine words

fine

line

mine

nine

vine

© 2001 Rigby Pebble Soup

## w words

want

wash

we

will

with

## -alk words

talk

<u>walk</u>

chalk

## -oke words

joke

poke

<u>woke</u>

broke

choke

## x words

ax

exit

## -ix words

fix

mix

six

## -ox words

box

fox

ox

## y words

yak

yell

yes

you

your

## -ard words

card

hard

yard

guard

## -arn words

barn

yarn

## z words

zero

zip

zone

## -est words

best

nest

rest

test

<u>z</u>est

## -oo words

boo

moo

too

<u>z</u>oo

shoo

# Aa

# Bb

# Cc

# Dd

# Ee

# Ff

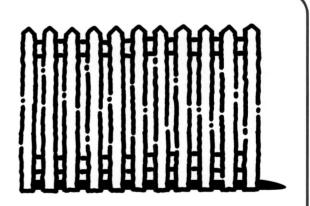

# Gg

# Hh

# I i

# J j

Jelly

# Kk

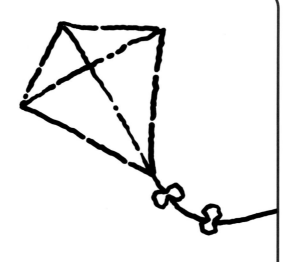

# Ll

# Mm

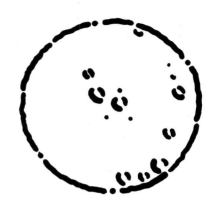

# Nn

# Oo

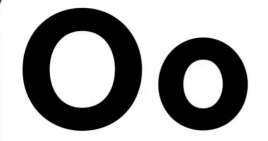

# Pp

# Qq

# Rr

# Ss

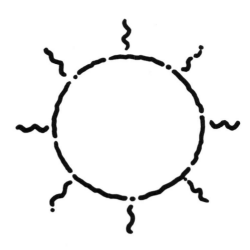

# Tt

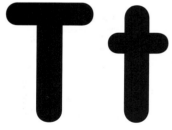

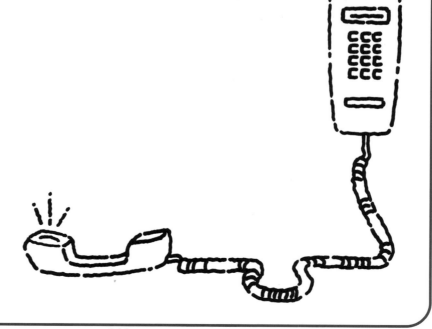

# U u

# V v

# W w

---

# X x

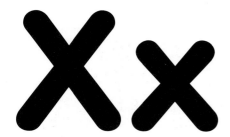

146

# Y y

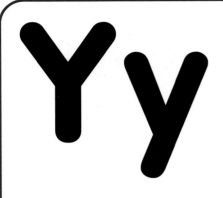

# Z z

Aa Bb Cc Dd Ee Ff

Gg Hh Ii Jj Kk Ll

Mm Nn Oo Pp Qq

Rr Ss Tt Uu Vv Ww

Xx Yy Zz